What the

"Dave Birss has na[something] *book about creativity. Not a surprise really. He has walked the walk and always talks a good talk. This book fuses his immense wisdom and his playful story-telling nature. Buy it. Read it. Practise it. Share it."*

Marc Lewis
Dean, School of Communication Arts

"Lucid and useful. Written with economy. Next time you get stuck, use it to get unstuck."

Alan Young & Julian Vizard
Creative Partners, St. Luke's

"The business world really needs to understand creativity. And Dave has got a ton of good stuff to add to the debate."

Steve Henry
Co-founder of Decoded & Creative Director

"Dave Birss rubbishes the notion that great ideas are 'plucked from the air'. His book looks at where ideas come from and shows how to boost our 'creativity'. He should charge a lot of money for it."

Lee Tan
Executive Creative Director, McCann

"The genius of this book is to debunk the myth that somehow the act of creation in whatever form is not a discipline. In my experience the greatest producers of all and any creativity I've encountered are as disciplined in the pursuit of their craft as an athlete is in the pursuit of their chosen sport."

Jim Thornton
Creative Director, VCCP

A User Guide to the Creative Mind

by Dave Birss

AN addi+ive PUBLICATION

An Additive Publication
www.getadditive.com
www.userguidetothecreativemind.com

First published in the UK by Additive

Copyright © 2012 by Additive

All rights reserved. No part of this publication may be reproduced or distributed in any form or by any means, or stored in a database or retrieval system, without the prior written permission of the copyright owner. If you're actually reading this, hello. How are you doing? We recommend you keep turning the pages because the good stuff is a few pages further on.

ISBN 978-1-4716-2098-0

Words by Dave Birss

Cover concept and design by John De Vries

Ever so slightly updated November 2013

Contents

- 1   WHAT THIS BOOK IS NOT
- 2   AUTHOR'S NOTE

- 5   **SECTION 1 - CREATIVITY TAKES WORK**
- 6   WHAT EXACTLY IS CREATIVITY?
- 8   WHAT IS A CREATIVE IDEA?
- 10   THE CREATIVE HABIT
- 12   THE CREATIVE PROCESS
- 14   INPUT
- 16   PROCESS
- 20   OUTPUT
- 22   NURTURE
- 24   CRAFT
- 26   AND IF THE IDEAS JUST AREN'T COMING?

29	**SECTION 2 - TRICKS OF THE MIND**
31	THE MIND IS A DELICATE TOOL
32	HIT THE PUB
33	GIVE YOURSELF A SOUNDTRACK
34	HIT THE PUB AGAIN
35	REWRITE THE PROBLEM
36	SOLVE A SUDOKU
37	BE AN ACTOR
38	BE REALLY DREADFUL
39	GO READ SOME STUFF
40	HAVE A NAP
41	MAP YOUR THOUGHTS
42	SET A GOAL
43	HIT ANOTHER PUB
45	**SECTION 3 - THE CREATIVE CHEAT SHEET**
48	WHAT'S THE LOGICAL CONCLUSION?
50	WHAT'S THE ILLOGICAL CONCLUSION?
52	BEAT UP THE ENEMY
54	USE THE MEDIUM

56	REMOVE ALL THE WORDS
58	REMOVE ALL THE PICTURES
60	PLAY WITH SCALE
62	CREATE A SKEWED WORLD
64	WHAT'S IT LIKE?
66	TELL THE TRUTH
68	PUT THE AUDIENCE IN THE IDEA
70	GO ON! PROVE IT!
72	USE A CELEBRITY
74	CELEBRATE THE PROBLEM
76	MAKE IT A GAME
78	SHOCK THE F**K OUT OF PEOPLE
82	ABOUT THE AUTHOR
85	ABOUT THE DESIGNER
86	READING LIST
89	BIG, BIG THANKS
91	ABOUT ADDITIVE
93	ABOUT ONE DAY CODE SCHOOL
95	FEED YOUR EARS

What this book is not

This book isn't a shortcut to hard work. It's a guide to help you understand the creative process, make more of your skills and direct your efforts in fruitful directions.

If you're looking for something that will turn your mind into a rainbow fountain of totally fresh and unexpected ideas, I would suggest you try extreme sleep deprivation or LSD.

The creative techniques at the end of the book aren't there to help you slack off. They're there to give you a nudge down some avenues you may not have looked at yet.

And this book is not just for advertising creatives. It's for anyone with an interest in understanding more about the murky world of creativity.

Arse covered. Let's move on.

Author's note

I never intended to write this book.

It's all thanks to Apple's iBooks Author application. I wanted to see what it's like to use, found it incredibly simple and decided to create something with it as a test. That test then led to this printed gem. Which is the exact opposite of the usual route.

The bones of this book were written more than 10 years ago when I was Deputy Creative Director of an ad agency called Mr Smith. Sadly, it was a short-lived agency that was Crispin Porter + Bogusky's European division. And it was my first proper crack at being part of a creative leadership team.

There were some juniors in the department who I wanted to help — so I started to put some of my thinking down on a laptop screen. I wrote a number of guides covering subjects like 'how to be more persuasive in your copy', 'how to write and interpret briefs', 'how to defend work' and the example that makes up the latter part of this book: 'the creative cheat sheet'.

I also put a couple of these guides up on the web, this one becoming the most popular. I've received emails from all over the world thanking me for it. And so — voila! — here it is in all its physical glory.

Please don't get me wrong; this book is not a how-to guide or a shortcut to creativity. Far from it! It started as a bottom-drawer, emergency kit for when you find yourself stuck in a rut. It's some of the techniques that I use myself when the deadline's tight and I'm suffering from the dreaded brain-freeze. Or a hangover.

To make the book more useful, I've added some of my thoughts on the creative process. Much of these come from my blog posts, other documents and talks that I've done on creativity.

Unsurprisingly, there are thoughts in here that other people have covered before me. Most notably James Webb Young in his wonderful 1965 book "A Technique for Producing Ideas". If you haven't got a copy, I highly recommend it. It's under 50 pages and only takes a few minutes to read. Perfect!

I'm pretty sure this guide will be publicly hated and privately loved by creatives. That's fine. I just hope that it's useful.

And I'm sure there are things in here that'll also be useful for people who don't make their living out of coming up with ideas to market stuff.

I just ask that if you do find it useful — or if you have any additions, amends or improvements — that you drop me a note to dave@getadditive.com

Big, big, big thanks,

Dave Birss
January 2012

Creativity takes work

What exactly is creativity?

The advertising industry uses the word all the time.

They turn it into a noun.

The call the adverts 'the creative'.

They call the people who come up with the adverts 'the creatives'.

They also use it as an adjective.

"That ad is really creative."

"We're looking for a more creative approach."

But what is creativity?

The popular misconception is that it's an innate ability that some people have and others don't. That these blesséd demigods sit back, pop their feet on the desk and wait for the muse to strike. They pluck ideas out of the ether like great conjurors. They're tormented and temperamental beasts with a rare and special talent.

That's bullcrap.

And, amazingly, a lot of advertising creatives seem to have fallen for it.

But all the best creatives know it isn't like that at all. It takes far more applied effort.

So I'd like to demystify things.

Creativity is a step by step process as much as making spaghetti bolognese is. And, like making that fine Italian staple, you can't just do the steps in any old order.

You need to start with the raw ingredients and do a fair amount of work before you end up with the good stuff.

We'll take a look at the creative process shortly.

What is a creative idea?

If you'll excuse me getting biblical on your ass, it says in Ecclesiastes:

> WHAT HAS BEEN WILL BE AGAIN,
> WHAT HAS BEEN DONE
> WILL BE DONE AGAIN;
> THERE IS NOTHING NEW
> UNDER THE SUN.

That was probably written in the 4th century BC. And nothing's really changed since then.

I used to think creativity was about true originality. About doing something that no one on the face of the planet has ever seen before. However, if you actually succeeded with that aim, your audience wouldn't have any reference for how to interpret what you'd produced. And that's not much good when you're trying to sell washing powder.

It's better to think of a creative idea as a recombination of existing elements.

Nowhere is this shown better than in the book 'George Lois on his Creation of the Big Idea'. Each spread shows where George got his inspiration from and shows how that helped him create an ad. Or a magazine cover.

It's just like what Jim Jarmusch said:

> IT'S NOT WHERE YOU TAKE IT FROM, IT'S WHERE YOU TAKE IT TO.

But you must remember to take it 'to' somewhere great.

There are too many people who settle for 'taking it from'.

Those people are plagiarists.

And you're not like that.

The creative habit

I believe that everyone has what it takes to be creative. But there are some people who just seem to excel at it.

Again, most people put it down to natural ability. And — who knows — there may be some genetic sequence that predisposes them to creative excellence. But the traits these people display are actually habits that can be developed by just about anyone.

They have an obsession with acquiring knowledge. They're able to become fascinated by just about any topic. So they probably spend more time on Wikipedia than the average Joe. But they're also easily distracted, so they don't disappear all the way down the rabbit hole. This results in an amazing breadth of knowledge with a few specialist areas of expertise. And it makes them pretty interesting people to hang out with at dinner parties.

They treat their mind the way a foodie treats their stomach: they fill it with good stuff. You'll often find them at museums, art galleries, the cinema, the theatre, bookshops and concerts.

That's because they understand that you need to put good stuff in if you want good stuff to come out.

It's not unusual to find them doing interesting things outside of their day job. I was one of three Creative Directors in a well respected agency a few years ago and all of us had other businesses on the side. One had a fashion label, another made products and I had a couple of web businesses.

If you want to be a truly great creative person, you need to cultivate these habits.

Because — as many great people have said before me — being creative isn't an occupation, it's a preoccupation.

The creative process

If the very notion of creativity being a process fills you with disgust, read no further.

From what I understand, the process follows these steps:

- Input
- Process
- Output
- Nurture
- Craft

We'll look at these in a bit more detail over the next few pages.

But let me just pause for a second and say that many creative people do their job well without understanding what it is they're actually doing. They have a process but they don't want to define it or understand it too much.

That's perfectly OK.

Many years ago, when I was a musician, I was jamming with a singer songwriter. I asked him what chord he had just played and he told me he didn't know. So I looked at his fingers and started to tell him what it was before he stopped me dead.

He didn't want to know.

To him, understanding the theory would kill the magic. It's clearly worked for him because the chap's name is Gary Lightbody and his band Snow Patrol seem to have done alright for themselves.

If what you're doing is working well, maybe you don't need to understand it.

And this book may just have been a waste of money.

Sorry about that.

No refunds.

Input

When I started in the industry it was quite common to do a factory visit. In my first few years I visited a number of whisky distilleries. On one occasion I was given a newly-launched car for a couple of weeks. And I even spent a few days in Scotland's highest security prison for dangerous offenders.

You did these things with the aim of getting to know the subject you were advertising as well as possible.

Thanks to tightening budgets and short-sightedness, these things don't seem to happen any more. But you still need to immerse yourself in the product as fully as you can.

Don't just rely on planners to condense the best stuff into the creative brief. Do your own research. Look at the nitty gritty. Because often the best insights are in the smallest of details. Little things other people assume are insignificant could be golden nuggets just waiting to be formed into a great idea. This is what Robin Wight would refer to as 'interrogating the product'. There's nearly always something in there if you look hard enough.

And because you need to combine these elements with other elements, you need to keep feeding your mind with lots of good stuff. Preferably stuff outside the world of advertising so that your work doesn't become derivative. The more inspiring stuff you have in the thought-bank, the better the chance you have of creating something truly great.

So now we've got a head full of facts and details and insights and inspiration, what do we do next?

Process

This is where you start to combine elements.

Take stuff from your research about the product and start to combine it with other elements to see what happens.

Try combining it with the mating rituals of the Puffin.

Or Handel's Messiah.

Or that scene from Pulp Fiction when everyone's pointing guns at each other.

Or a piece of Ndebele art.

Just like chemistry, things start to happen when you combine elements. Sometimes you get something brown and icky. And other times you get a dramatic explosion.

These other elements are commonly known as 'inspiration'. Most people just sit there and wait for this inspiration to hit them out of the blue. By actively combining elements, you've more chance of finding the right inspiration for the job.

And, again, here it's clear why those people who are in the habit of feeding their mind produce better work.

You'll generally find that you produce quite a lot of stuff at the start. But as you go on, your pace will slow and you'll run aground. The ideas will stop coming. You'll think that you've done as much as you can possibly do and you should maybe stop where you are.

There lies the path to mediocrity.

I suggest that at this point you persevere.

Do your best to push through the barrier and you'll hit another flow of ideas. And then you'll run dry again. Your head will be in a spin and you won't be able to think straight.

That's exactly where you want to be.

Now it's time to walk away and put your mind on something else.

Doodle on your pad.

Do a Sudoku.

Play some music.

Go to an art gallery.

Have a sleep.

All that stuff moves the thinking from the conscious front part of the brain to the more powerful back part of the brain. (Don't quote me on that — I know next to nothing about neuropsychology!)

Now you need to let it brew.

And brew.

And brew.

Output

Then, all being well, you'll be struck with a bolt of inspirational lightning.

It'll probably happen at a time you don't expect it.

Like in the middle of the night.

When you're having a shower.

When you're waiting for a bus.

It will often happen when you don't have a notepad.

Hopefully, it will happen more than once.

You should take a seat and jot it all down. As you do so, other ideas will fall out. This is the magical part of the process. And this is what people associate with those moments of creative genius.

But you couldn't have got here without all the previous work.

Now what do we do with these unpolished nuggets?

Nurture

You've got a collection of ideas from throughout the process now.

Some of these came from your 'eureka' moment and some of them came when you were trying to combine elements.

Evaluate them. Do they fit the brief? Do they do what you're being asked to do? Some of them will almost certainly hit the bin. Others may need some adjustments. Others may not exactly fit the brief but are just too fantastic to ditch.

Don't be afraid to share them with people. If you work with good people, they'll add to your idea. (The wrong kind of people will poke holes and make your idea smaller.

These are people you don't want to be working with.)

Make no mistake, you've not arrived yet. There's still some work to be done. You need to spend time growing and developing those ideas.

Try playing with the tone of the copy.

Try playing with the balance of the layout.

Turn it all upside down and see how it feels.

Look at the interaction and transitions in your digital work.

Again, the inspiration you've gathered from the real world can play a big role here. Animation styles, photographic techniques, new technology, colour palettes.

Take your best ideas and make them better.

Don't skimp.

The extra effort is what separates the good from the great.

Craft

Once you've got your fantastic chosen idea and — hopefully — the client's bought it, you need to make it as good as it can be.

You need to have stamina here.

You need to make sacrifices.

And you need to have high standards.

If you want this to be great, you're going to be saying 'no' a lot.

Your creative problem solving skills will move from creating and crafting ideas to coming up with work-arounds for issues. Like not having a big enough budget. Or hitting a technical issue. Or having another pressing job that's encroaching on your time.

There's a certain amount of the crafting that you'll be doing yourself. These are learned skills. If you don't feel you have those skills personally, ask for the help of somebody who does. And learn from them as they do it. Great creative people never stop picking up new things.

However, some of this final process needs to be done by other suppliers. Make sure you have the best people you can afford. You want them to put as much love into it as you have. You want them to see your vision and be aiming for the same level of wondrousness.

It would be such a shame to have come so far only to fall at the last hurdle.

And if the ideas just aren't coming?

Not everyone can be creative every day.

Sometimes it just doesn't happen for whatever reason.

But 'just not feeling it today' doesn't look good on a timesheet.

So the next couple of sections are designed to help you deal with that.

The first one is about how to get your mind in the right state for being creative.

And the second section offers you a number of different creative approaches you can try out.

I've collected a few of the techniques that I use personally to give my thinking a bit of a nudge. And I've added some examples of recent creative work to illustrate each technique.

These aren't exhaustive. And I'm sure many of you will have your own methods. (If you do, please drop me an email to tell me about them. I may include them in the next update.)

I don't recommend you use these as a regular crutch. That'll lead to formulaic work. Which is the opposite of creative work.

But before we get to that, let's take a look inside your head.

Tricks of the mind

When you find yourself stagnating,
try these.

The mind is a delicate tool

The human brain is the most remarkable creation in nature.

That one organ has shaped so much of the world around us. Most items in the room you're sitting in. The composition of the air you're breathing. The very stack of paper you hold in your hands right now.

But it's also an amazingly fragile tool.

It's governed by emotions rather than logic.

And that means you'll often find it doesn't work properly.

Here are some techniques that might help to get it moving again.

Hit the pub

Or an art gallery.

Or the park.

Or the jacuzzi. (This is my personal favourite. I've got a collection of wrinkled notebooks!)

Changing location also changes your emotional state and gives you a new perspective on things.

I've always had difficulty doing creative work in an office. As a result, I've often encouraged creatives to go somewhere more inspiring to work.

I don't care if I see them at their desk as long as I see good ideas.

Give yourself a soundtrack

Cows that listen to soothing music produce more milk.

Different tempos and styles of music put us in different emotional states.

Baroque music, for example, generally has a tempo that's similar to the speed of the brainwaves associated with creative thinking.

I'm not sure about Ricky Martin.

Just in general.

Hit the pub again

Go for a pint.

Or, if it's too early for that, have a coffee.

If you're a filthy smoker, indulge your habit.

These relaxants and stimulants change the way your mind operates.

But too much of them will give you other problems.

[Insert Surgeon General's warning here]

Rewrite the problem

It may be that the way your problem is phrased isn't inspiring you.

Find other ways of expressing it.

Maybe even as a picture.

The best way to find the right solution is to make sure you're asking the right question.

Solve a Sudoku instead

It could just be that your mind is too close to the problem.

If your brain is all a-jumble and you can't get it clear, do something that requires conscious thought.

At that point your conscious brain hands the problem over to your unconscious brain to detangle. And it's good at that.

It also gives you a bit of distance from the problem and helps to put it in perspective.

Plus, Sudoku is good brain exercise. And you don't want a flabby cerebellum, do you?

Be an actor

If you're not sure you've got the abilities to solve the problem in front of you, pretend you're someone else.

How would Stephen Fry approach it?

Or Batman?

Or Leonardo Da Vinci?

Or Sarah Silverman?

Put yourself in their shoes and you may find you've got abilities you never knew you had.

Be really dreadful

Sometimes your expectations are so high that it puts too much pressure on you. You need to chill out or you'll not come up with anything at all.

If you're worried about your ideas not being good enough, set yourself the challenge of coming up with really, really bad ideas.

It gets your mind moving and can be loads of fun.

And in the process of coming up with total dross, you may find some good ideas falling out as well.

Just remember to reset your standard to 'high' after you get things moving!

Go read some stuff

Read the brief.

Read research.

Read user manuals.

Read the collected poetry of Oscar Wilde.

Read this book again.

You need to feed your mind with all the right information. And you may have overlooked a hidden gem in the brief that leads to a great thought.

Or something unrelated to the task in hand may inspire you in another direction.

If you don't put the good stuff in, you won't get good stuff out.

Have a nap

Each time I've started at a new agency, I've scoured the building for a place to go for a sneaky snooze.

Once I built a green-screen film studio in the basement of an agency. So I used to go there for power naps. But I couldn't tell anyone about it. They wouldn't have understood.

The thought of going to sleep during work hours is sadly frowned upon. But I'm a big believer in it.

A 15 minute snooze can do you much more good than just sitting at your desk getting frustrated.

In fact, I think I'm going to do that right now before I write the next section.

Map your thoughts

If you want to see that you're covering sufficient territory, draw it down in the form of a mind map.

I do this quite regularly.

I draw a circle (more like an untidy oval) in the centre of a sheet of paper and I write the problem or proposition in it.

I then draw spider's legs outwards, with each one representing a different area of thought.

These sometimes form their own nodes with additional legs leading to executional ideas.

It usually ends up an ugly mess. But it makes it easier to see if your thinking has been broad enough.

Set a goal

Years ago, when I was trying to get a placement at an agency, the Creative Director handed me a brand new layout pad, a couple of markers and a brief. And he told me to come back in 48 hours having filled every single page with ideas.

It seemed like an unsurmountable challenge.

But I did it.

And I got the placement.

Set yourself a goal like that.

Make your aim quantity rather than quality. You're bound to dig up some good stuff along the way.

Hit another pub

And talk to people this time.

If you've got some ideas, share them with a friend. And listen to what they have to say about them.

Or find a stranger, buy them a drink and ask them some questions. Think of it as enjoyable market research.

Just don't isolate yourself.

Your idea is going to have to work in the real world, so let it meet an audience early on.

The Creative Cheat Sheet

For when you need something more
to kick you out of the rut.

I've been working as a creative for nearly 20 years. And there have been plenty of times when my muse has stubbornly refused to play ball.

However, the deadline hasn't allowed for that.

So here are some of the techniques I use to hotwire the creative side of my brain.

What's the logical conclusion?

Be sensible.

Be logical.

If what you're being asked to say is true, it'll have consequences.

Try changing the focus of the brief.

If you've been asked to say that a car is fuel-efficient, change your proposition to the fact that it saves you money; or it prevents you from having to make too many stops at a petrol station; or it makes the fuel gauge a very boring thing to look at.

If your proposition is about a cure for the common cold think about the doctor's surgery being empty; or a doctor being bored in their office; or a supermarket doing a special on their surplus order of hankies; or someone having to come up with a better excuse to pull a sickie.

What's the illogical conclusion?

Be nonsensical.

Be ridiculous.

If you were Wile E. Coyote, there would be an entirely different outcome.

Now it's time to step into the world of cartoon.

You've been given a brief for an incredibly fuel efficient car again. This time you're going to be a bit daft with your solutions.

If you start thinking like Homer Simpson, the proposition could now mean that you forget where the petrol cap is because it's so long since you've used one; the only thing you refuel at the service station is yourself when you buy some donuts; petrol stations start going out of business because so many people are buying this car.

These are unbelievably wild outcomes but they help to illustrate the proposition in a more entertaining way.

Beat up the enemy

Don't hold back.

Knock the living crap out of them!

*Find their weak point and
get to work.*

Is your product better than the competition? Even in just one way?

Show people how your product compares favourably. Do a good-old-fashioned side by side comparison to show how your product stacks up. Or, if it can be done in an acceptable way, rip the competition to shreds.

Or how about attacking the audience's nemesis? Who or what could stop them getting what they want?

Or is there a common enemy for both the brand and the audience? Fighting against the same cause is a great way of creating unity.

Whoever it is, don't hold back.

Use the medium

Marshall McLuhan famously said: "The medium is the message."

Take him at his word.

Utilise the space you've got to aid what you're saying.

Is the space where the ad's going to appear of any help?

Is it an unusual size or shape?

Where will it appear?

What will it be surrounded by?

Can you use a quirk of the media to communicate the message?

Your visual may just be the ad itself.

Remove all
the words

~~This space is intentionally left blank.~~

See if you can do the whole job in the visual without a headline. It's the ultimate distillation of communication.

Sir John Hegarty apparently put a screensaver on the computers at BBH which read 'Words are a barrier to communication'.

He may just have a point.

So how would you get the message across to a person who can't read? Or what would it look like if it was a road sign? Aim for doing the whole job in the visual and if you end up having to chuck in a few words, at least your ad will be simpler.

Remove all the pictures

There aren't any images in this book.

But hopefully you're still getting something out of it.

In case you're having difficulty, I left some space below for you to draw a picture of a man with a typewriter.

Duke Ellington famously declared that "words stink up the place". That's true if they're written by someone whose writing stinks. However, great writing has the power to change the world.

How would you convince someone if the only way to reach them was to write a letter?

How would you make your point if you were writing a film monologue for Robert De Niro?

Or a speech for Winston Churchill?

Ditch the picture and use a thousand words.

Play with scale

Exaggerate.

Make small things big.

Make big things small.

Expand, contract, reduce, enlarge.

Blow it all out of proportion.

Things feel different when you alter their size.

The tiny bottles of booze you get in minibars always make me smile. Especially when I've emptied them.

And I often find myself attracted to the giant packs of Marlboro cigarettes in airport duty free shops. Even although I don't smoke.

Do the same with the problem.

Make a small issue insurmountable.

Make a mediocre benefit life-changingly awesome.

Or make a complicated thing totally simple.

Create a skewed world

Create a world that's just like ours — but slightly different.

Magic can happen.

Gravity can switch off.

Everyone is permanently happy.

You don't need to limit yourself to what's possible. That's dull. People are used to that.

Introduce them to a different world. One that shows the product in a different light.

If you're selling car insurance, you could have all cars designed like bumper cars. And people are smiling and enjoying themselves just driving down the street. That would let you talk about the fact that life isn't quite like that and a little prang with another car is a truly miserable experience.

If you're selling a face cleansing cream, you could have a world where people's faces actually glow with light. They use them to read books in the dark and illuminate cupboards. That represents the inner radiance that the product reveals.

It just has to be noticeably different.

And totally brilliant.

What's it like?

Everything's a bit like something else

Either the way it looks.

Or the way it works.

Or the way it makes us feel.

Embrace the similar.

Are there any metaphors for the product?

Is it like a lion or a camel or a clockwork chicken?

Is it a Harley Davidson rider wearing drag?

Or a car that runs on custard?

Or a dolphin with an aqualung?

Metaphors are great ways of helping the audience understand something in a simple way. But it's easy for them to be cheesy so be careful to avoid clichés. Please! If I see another image of a zebra amongst horses as an analogy of how a company stands out from the crowd, I think I'll borrow a metaphorical rifle and climb a metaphorical clocktower.

Tell the truth

McCann Erickson's motto is: "Truth Well Told".

Yet most people think advertising is a pack of lies.

Prove them wrong.

Dramatically.

Revolutionary, or what?

Most people have a healthy distrust of advertising, so being blatantly honest can have a dramatic effect.

Look at the old classic Avis campaign — 'We're number two, so we try harder'. Genius! They hit you with something so surprisingly truthful in the first half of the phrase that you have little option but to believe the second half.

Or how about Skoda's advertising? They never tried to hide the fact that they had a stinking image. Instead, they capitalised on it. The whole campaign was even stronger because it was backed up by award-winning products. It convinced me enough to go out and buy one, anyway.

Put the audience in the idea

The direct marketing industry has been doing personalisation for years.

But digital technology lets us take it to a whole new level.

Many people are saying this is the age of 'mass personalisation'.

Embrace those new opportunities.

If you're anything like me, you'll respond better to a letter with your name on it than one that starts 'to whom it may concern'.

You'll listen to people who know a bit more about you than those who generically imagine you're just like the average punter in your demographic.

You'll be more interested in listening to someone if they're interested in listening to you.

You'll be more interested in something if some of your friends have already taken part.

That's life.

And that's one of the great things it's been too difficult to do up until now.

Go on! Prove it!

If that ballsy product claim is a fact, you must be able to demonstrate it.

In a dramatic way, of course.

If you've got a strong proposition stating how your product is better than the rest, prove it.

But do it in an interesting and surprising way.

Could you show your washing up liquid cleaning a truck full of plates as well as the truck?

Could you show your car beating an F-15 fighter jet along a runway?

Could you pile up coins higher than a house to demonstrate exactly how much your mortgage will save someone in the next 12 months?

Demonstrations have been used since the dawn of advertising. But that doesn't mean they're out of date. Just remember two things: keep them honest and make them dramatic.

Use a celebrity

There's a world full of A, B, C and D list celebs out there just ready to sell their soul for some cash.

But please use them creatively.

Please.

I hate this one. But it may just work for you.

Please, please, please don't use a celebrity just for the sake of it.

Borrowed interest is only useful if it actively builds on a strong concept.

Unfortunately, when the latest fast-rising celebrity appears, they are usually over-exploited by advertisers. And their agents know they've got a limited shelf-life so it's a good idea to make money while they can.

Some people would call it 'selling out'.

There are some examples of great ads with big names. But I'm sorry to say that they are the exception to the rule.

This is the route many agencies choose when they don't have a decent idea.

Tread carefully. It can suck big time.

Celebrate the problem

Problems can be good.

It all depends on how you look at things.

Being too famous to go out in public is something many kids dream of.

Being too damn sexy is another.

Believe me, it's not as good as it sounds.

What is the issue that your product resolves?

Maybe your product frees you up to enjoy that problem all the more.

This worked great for Persil with their 'dirt is good' campaign because getting dirty can be lots of fun. Especially if you're 8 years old. Or drunk. So rather than stifle that opportunity for enjoyment — do it more and let Persil deal with the consequences.

This strategy will work great for products like hangover cures, liposuction and genital wart cream.

But not so great for chemotherapy, psychiatric treatments and prosthetic limbs.

Make it a game

People play games all the time.

The most mundane activities are more fun when you make them playable.

Like trying to get the skin off an apple in one single peel.

Or not stepping on pavement cracks.

We just can't help it.

One of the big buzzwords of the last couple of years has been 'gamification'. It's the understanding that we naturally turn things into games.

Even dull pencil-pushers turn their repetitive drudgery into little games. They'll try to get all the documents in their out- tray totally straight. Or they'll play an internal betting game about how many documents they can process before 4.15.

It's natural. So embrace it.

Games are great ways of getting people excited and giving them the thrill of a reward.

They can be played solo. Or against other members of a community. Or against the world.

Let the games begin.

Shock the F**K out of people

Up yours!

I can't be arsed writing anything here.

Is there a visual you can use that will provoke a strong reaction?

Or could you say something that would seriously offend your parents?

If you're advertising an amazingly powerful vacuum cleaner, you could use a close-up shot of a dustmite – they scare the shit out of me!

If you're advertising a rugged bike helmet, you could show the mashed up corpse of a cyclist with tyre tracks across his chest and not even a scratch on the helmet.

If you're advertising underwear you could dress a goat up in it and say that bestiality is a serious option now.

Remember that it's OK to upset the people you're not selling to. And sometimes the right thing is just to be plain wrong.

_____

....
....
_____

Come up with your own technique.

Then write about it here.

If it's any good, email it to me and it may end up in a future version of the book.

About the author

Dave Birss is a restless man.

He's worked in every area of the advertising industry, producing TV ads, radio campaigns, press, posters, direct mail, signage, sales promotions, experiences, digital stuff and those crappy little ads you get on the top of petrol pump handles.

He never quite decided whether he's an Art Director or a Copywriter, which led him to being both Head of Art and Head of Copy at different agencies.

He's picked up a bunch of awards across different disciplines.

He's been a creative lead at a number of agencies, including OgilvyOne, Poke and McCann Worldgroup.

These days he spends much of his time helping organizations to increase their creativity through his company Additive.

He also runs One Day Code School to teach the languages of the web in a single day.

When he finds the time, he hosts the Future of Advertising podcast where he interviews the biggest names in the industry to find out where they think things are going. (You can subscribe to it on iTunes.)

You can often find him talking at conferences around the world.

He mentors at the wonderful School of Communication Arts.

He's currently working on several other books.

And a handful of TV shows.

He lives in London with his wonderful wife and daughter.

He'd like you to get in touch.

He'll try his very best to respond to you.

He's nice that way.

Here's his email address:

dave@getadditive.com

About the designer

John De Vries is a multi award-winning art director and designer based in Amsterdam.

He's worked for some great agencies, including DDB&Co, JWT and Doom & Dickson. Now BBDO are benefitting from his wonderful Art Direction skills.

Just for the fun of it, he came up with the cover concept and designed the heck out of it. That makes him equally talented, lovely and mad.

If this book makes it into the New York Times bestseller list, I'm flying him to London for dinner at the Ritz.

Reading list

There are a lot of books that cover some of this material better than I ever could. I'd consider many of these to be essential reading for anyone who wants to get good at coming up with ideas.

So here are some helpful additions for you library. Although, sadly, some of the books appear to be out of print:

A Technique for Producing Ideas
James Webb Young

Lateral Thinking
Edward De Bono

George Lois on his Creation of the Big Idea
George Lois

The Craft Of Copywriting
Alastair Crompton

The D&AD Copy Book
D&AD

The D&AD Art Direction book
D&AD

How To Do Better Creative Work
Steve Harrison

Hegarty on Advertising
John Hegarty

Creative Mischief
Dave Trott

The Advertising Concept Book
Pete Barry

Creativity Now
Jurgen Wolff

Creative Advertising: Ideas and Techniques
Mario Pricken

Hey, Whipple, Squeeze This
Luke Sullivan

Whatever You Think, Think the Opposite
Paul Arden

Big, big thanks

To my amazingly tolerant and supportive wife and daughter. They put up with my ridiculous projects and impulsive whims without so much as a grumble.

To my parents for encouraging me to follow my heart.

To Marc Lewis at the School of Communication Arts for his support.

To Al Young and Julian Vizard at St. Luke's for making the book bigger.

To Holly Brockwell for volunteering her excellent proofreading skills.

To John De Vries for a great cover design.

To all the far-more talented people than me who read through the manuscript and helped to make it better.

And to you for just being you.

About Additive

Additive work with organizations to help them boost their creativity.

We do that in a number of ways, including teaching creative techniques, developing a creative culture, looking at internal processes, spotting opportunities and inspiring people to come up with fresh and innovative ideas.

We are based in London but work all over the world.

You can find out more about us at:

getadditive.com

Or, even better, you can reach us at:

hello@getadditive.com

Learn web languages at One Day Code School

If you have anything to do with the internet, it's a good idea to understand a bit of the lingo.

This course takes you from little or no understanding of code to building your very own website in just 8 hours.

You'll leave with a good understanding of HTML and CSS. As well as knowledge of how and when to use JavaScript. You'll have a better understanding of how to deal with developers. And you'll get our exclusive book to remind you of everything you learned during the day.

Find out more about the course at:

onedaycodeschool.com

Feed your ears

Dave Birss hosts the Future of Advertising podcast.

In each show, he talks to an advertising legend to find out where they think the industry's going.

Recent guests include George Lois, Sir John Hegarty, Dave Trott, Robin Wight, Billy Mawhinney, Tony Brignull, Rory Sutherland, Cindy Gallup and Paul Brazier.

And he's got plenty more legends waiting in the wings.

You can find out more at:

FutureOfAdvertising.info

And you can subscribe on iTunes.

Thanks for reading.

Now visit:

UserGuideToTheCreativeMind.com

Printed in Great Britain
by Amazon